COLIN POWELL

Straight to the Top

by Rose Blue and
Corinne J. Naden

The Millbrook Press
Brookfield, Connecticut
A Gateway Biography
Updated Edition

Cover photographs courtesy of Black Star ©1993 John Harrington

Photographs courtesy of: Department of Defense: pp. 4, 24 (both), 31, 35; Wide World Photos, Inc.: pp. 7, 18 (both), 37 (both); Marilyn Powell Berns: pp. 11, 12; Conrad Waldinger: p. 15; Library of Congress: p. 21 (top); UPI/Bettmann: p. 21 (bottom, both); Black Star, © Dennis Brack: p. 28; Pete Souza/Gamma Liaison: p. 41. Map by Robert Italiano, courtesy of Blackbirch Graphics

Library of Congress Cataloging-in-Publication Data
Blue, Rose.
Colin Powell : straight to the top / by Rose Blue and Corinne J. Naden.
p.   cm. — (A Gateway biography)
Includes index.
Summary: Profiles the life of the distinguished general, from his early life, to his involvement in the Persian Gulf War, to his evolving political career.
ISBN 0-7613-0256-5 (lib. bdg.). — ISBN 0-7613-0242-5 (pbk.)
1. Powell, Colin L. 2. Afro-American generals—Biography—Juvenile literature. 3. Generals—United States—Biography—Juvenile literature. 4. United States. Army—Biography—Juvenile literature. [1. Powell, Colin L. 2. Generals. 3. Afro-Americans—Biography.] I. Naden, Corinne J. II. Title. III. Series.
E840.5.P68B57   1997
355'.0092—dc21   [B]   96-39006   CIP   AC

From Rose: Dedicated to Dr. James Bell,
who is dedicated to the children,
one of those who "paved the way."

From Corinne: To my cousins Mary Lou
and Artie Wiesner, with love.

The authors thank Robert De Marshe
for his guidance through the maze of
Bronx streets and for his patience in
finding landmarks that pertained to
General Powell. Our thanks also to
Mitchell Strear for the ROTC photo
and for his help.

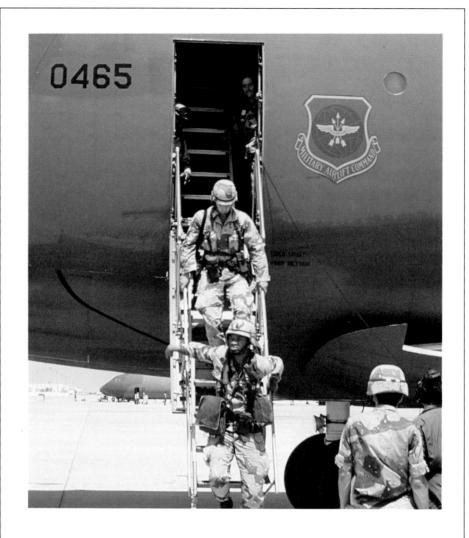

U.S. troops arrive in Saudi Arabia in 1990, before the outbreak of the Persian Gulf War. They were sent after Iraq invaded the oil-rich country of Kuwait.

On *August 2, 1990,* Iraq invaded and conquered Kuwait. The news shocked the world. Kuwait is on the Persian Gulf, sandwiched between Iraq to the north and west and Saudi Arabia to the south. This is part of the troubled area called the Middle East.

Oil-rich Kuwait is a tiny desert land that is only a little larger than the state of Connecticut. Overpowered by Iraq, Kuwait asked the United Nations (U.N.) for help. Saudi Arabia, afraid of being invaded next, also turned to the world organization. The United Nations said Iraq was wrong. To protect Saudi Arabia, President George Bush sent U.S. troops there. This was the start of Operation Desert Shield. The U.S. forces were soon joined by troops from Britain, France, Egypt, and other U.N. members.

During the next few months, many countries urged Iraq to leave Kuwait. Iraq's leader, Saddam Hussein, refused. Finally, the United Nations ordered Iraq to get out of Kuwait by January 15, 1991. War was threatened.

January 15 came and went. Iraq did not budge.

One day later, on January 16, Operation Desert Shield turned into Operation Desert Storm. The United States and its allies went to war against Iraq.

The war became known as the Persian Gulf War. The allied forces numbered more than half a million. Most were U.S. troops. They faced an even larger Iraqi army. The Americans were fighting a war in a desert thousands of miles from home.

Even before the first shot was fired, President Bush counted on the help of his top military adviser, the chairman of the Joint Chiefs of Staff (JCS). The JCS includes the top people in all the branches of the U.S. military. The chairman that President Bush counted on was a four-star general in the U.S. Army. His name is Colin Luther Powell.

As chairman of the JCS, Colin Powell was the highest-ranking military officer in the United States and the world's most powerful soldier. He was fifty-two years old when he took over as chairman on October 1, 1989. That made him the youngest chairman ever. He was also the first African American to have this job.

Colin Luther Powell is an impressive person. He stands six feet, one inch tall and weighs two hun-

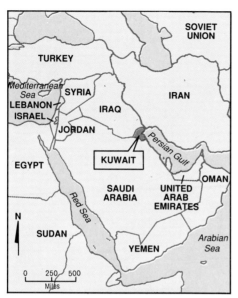

Kuwait and
the Middle East.

*As the highest-ranking officer
in the U.S. military, General
Colin Powell played a major
role in the 1991 Persian
Gulf War. Here he briefs
members of the press on
operations during the war.*

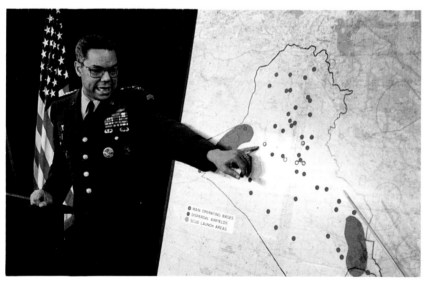

dred pounds. His dark, close-cropped hair is graying. It is said (although probably not to his face) that he has "teddy bear" good looks. His husky frame is held straight. He *looks* like a general.

Powell is every inch the military professional. He is quiet, serious, and businesslike. His manner is polished and even-tempered. He also has a sense of humor, and he can talk to civilians and military people with the same ease.

Powell was born into a poor immigrant family. How did he rise to become the country's top military man? There was no magic shortcut. Powell once said, "People keep asking the secret of my success. There isn't any secret. I work hard and spend long hours. It's as simple as that." He advised young people, "There is no substitute for hard work and study. Nothing comes easy."

T*hings were not easy* for young Colin Powell. He was born in Harlem in New York City on April 5, 1937. When Colin was still a child, his family moved to the South Bronx, another part of New York City. He grew up in a four-bedroom apartment on Kelly Street.

The South Bronx was, and still is, a poor neighborhood. Colin's mother and father came to America in the 1920s from the island of Jamaica in the Caribbean. Both parents worked in the garment district of New York City. Maud, Colin's mother, was a seamstress. Luther, his father, was a shipping clerk.

Colin Powell grew up to be a serious, strong military leader. But tears can still cloud his eyes when he speaks of his mother and father. They both died in the 1980s. "As I grow older," he has said, "I have greater and greater affection for my parents."

Maud and Luther Powell were serious people with a dream. They wanted a better life for Colin and his sister, Marilyn, who is five and a half years older than Colin. For the Powells, education was the key to a better life. Colin's mother graduated from high school; his father did not. If Maud Powell got annoyed at her husband, she would remind him just *who* had the high school diploma.

The Powells taught their children that success comes with hard work. "You must set a goal and do your job well," they said.

A reporter once suggested that Colin Powell got to the top because his parents taught him values. The general had this reply: "Kids don't pick up training because parents sit around and talk to them about values. Children watch their parents *live* values. Youngsters don't care about what you say, but they watch what you do."

The future general grew up in a warm, loving, hardworking family. His sister, Marilyn, remembers that when the family first moved to the South Bronx, there were few children his age in the neighborhood. So Colin went everywhere with her. "He was a tagalong brother," she says. She recalls that he was "really a pretty average boy," but he always "had a sense of direction." She was not surprised by his later success, only by the "greatness of it." Today Marilyn Powell Berns is married and is a teacher in Santa Ana, California.

The neighborhood around Kelly Street included people of many kinds. There were blacks and Puerto Ricans, and there was a large Jewish population. As Colin grew older, he played stickball on the streets with friends. He served as an altar boy at St. Margaret's Episcopal Church.

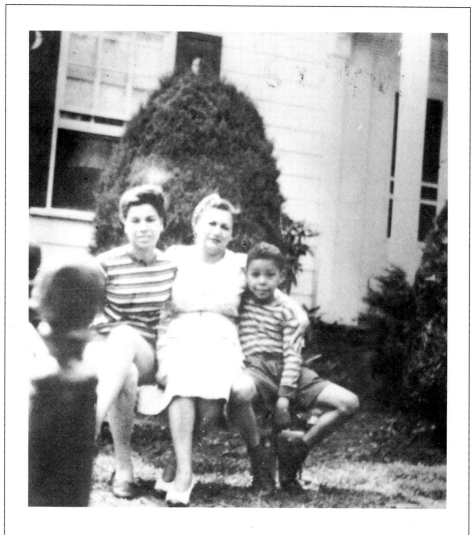

Colin grew up in a warm, close-knit family.
Here he is shown at about age seven, with his
mother and his sister, Marilyn.

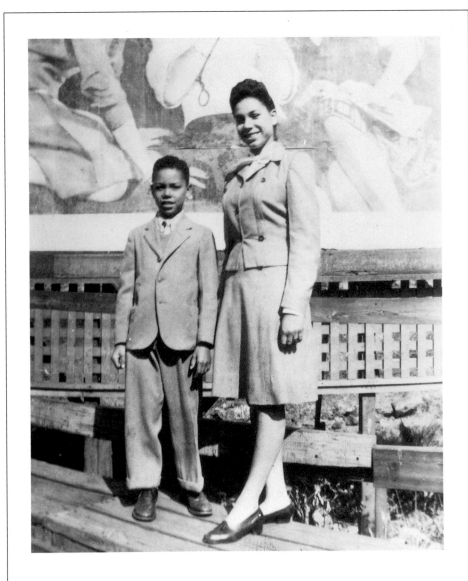

Colin, age eight, and Marilyn, age fourteen.

And, of course, he went to school—first to the neighborhood elementary school, and then to Morris High School nearby. After school, he worked at a furniture store in his neighborhood. He learned a little of the Yiddish language from the store's Jewish owners. "I had a great childhood," he later recalled.

Colin was not an honor student. He admits he sometimes "horsed around" at school. Colin Powell gives hope to all people who are C students. That was his grade average during high school and college.

Powell went to City College of New York (CCNY) in 1954. The school is now part of City University of New York (CUNY). He had no career in mind, but City College was free to New York students. He worked part-time after classes.

In his second semester of college, Powell joined the Reserve Officers Training Corps (ROTC). This program trains college students to become officers in the army. Powell's group was known as the Pershing Rifles. He later said that he joined because he liked the uniform. Actually, the military had always impressed him. He was a young boy during World War II and a teenager during the Korean War.

According to an old saying, some people "find a home in the army." In other words, sometimes a person is just right for military life. Colin Powell and the army seemed just right together. This C student got straight A's in his ROTC classes in all four years of college. When his group took summer training at Fort Bragg, North Carolina, he was named "outstanding cadet." It seems he had found a "home" in the army.

Powell earned a degree in geology (the study of the history of the Earth, especially through rocks) from CCNY in 1958. He graduated at the top of his ROTC group. He was a Pershing Rifles company commander, a cadet colonel (ROTC's highest rank), and a "distinguished military graduate."

One of Powell's ROTC classmates at CCNY was Mitchell Strear, who later became a school principal in New York City. Strear recalls: "Even back then Colin drew attention when he entered a room. At the age of eighteen, his bearing, manner, and presence were special. You just knew he would become a leader. The infantry has a motto: 'Follow me.' Colin's manner of acceptance of responsibility and leadership all said 'Follow me.'"

*Powell's Reserve Officers Training Corps (ROTC) unit,
the Pershing Rifles, posed for this picture in 1958. Powell
is in the top row, fifth from the left. He was a cadet colonel,
the highest rank in the ROTC.*

Powell decided to follow the army. On June 9, 1958, he became a second lieutenant. He earned sixty dollars a week. His parents encouraged him. They felt that, like most young men at the time, he would have been drafted into the military anyway. The Powells thought that their son would serve a tour of duty, then come home and get a "real job." Instead, he went into the army to stay. To him, a career in the military was "an honorable profession and a contribution to society."

But success in the military was not certain for Powell. In his profession, the most successful people have usually come from "the Point"—the U.S. Military Academy at West Point, New York. Many famous American generals were West Pointers. They include President Dwight D. Eisenhower and General Douglas MacArthur, who fought in World War II, and Robert E. Lee and Ulysses S. Grant, both generals in the Civil War.

General Colin Powell once said: "Although I had to compete in my military schooling with West Pointers . . . my CCNY foundation was so solid, I never regretted going anywhere but to City."

Lieutenant Powell was sent to training school at Fort Benning, Georgia. At that time, blacks and whites were segregated—kept apart by law—in many places. In the South, blacks were required to attend separate schools, which were generally not as good as the schools for whites. Blacks ate at segregated restaurants, sat in separate sections on buses and in movie theaters, and drank from separate water fountains.

Late in the 1950s, that was beginning to change. Blacks all over the country were beginning to demand, and win, civil rights—the basic rights of all citizens. But many whites still wanted the races to be kept separate. Thus, when Colin Powell went to Fort Benning at the age of twenty-one, he felt the shock of racism for the first time.

"On Kelly Street in the South Bronx, everybody was a minority," Powell later said. "I didn't know what a 'majority' was." But he realized his status soon enough. When he stopped at a restaurant in Columbus, Georgia, the waitress refused to serve him a hamburger unless he went to the back door.

Even after he became the army's top man, Powell never forgot how much blacks had suffered.

*In the 1950s,
segregation was
widespread in the
South. Top: A sign
points to a railway
waiting room for
blacks in Mississippi.
Bottom: Soldiers
block black students
from an all-white
high school in Little
Rock, Arkansas,
in 1957.*

He became a student of black history and an admirer of Martin Luther King, Jr., who led the civil rights struggle in the 1950s and 1960s. Powell has advised young African Americans: "Don't let your blackness, your minority status, be a problem to you. Let it be a problem to somebody else. . . . Beat them at it. Prove they're wrong. If you work hard, do the best you can, take advantage of every opportunity that's put in front of you, success will come your way."

In his own career, Powell has done just that. "In the army," he once said, "I never felt I was looked down on by my white colleagues. I've been given the opportunity to compete fair and square with them." It helped, he added, that he "came along at a time of change, a time of growth in civil rights."

African Americans have fought with honor in all of America's wars. But the military has not always treated them so honorably. Blacks fought in the American Revolution, but many were slaves. During the War of 1812 against the British, blacks fought in the Battle of New Orleans. But General Andrew Jackson had to argue with the government before they were paid.

Black troops fought in the Civil War, in World War I, and in World War II. They served bravely and well. But they were segregated—in separate fighting units, separate officers' clubs, and separate jobs. Men who cooked or served food to officers, for instance, were nearly always black.

In 1948, after World War II, President Harry S. Truman signed Executive Order 9981. It officially ended segregation in the armed forces. But the problem didn't go away overnight. There was still racism. But today there is no segregation in any of the U.S. armed services.

Besides Colin Powell, a number of blacks have had outstanding military careers. During World War II, Benjamin O. Davis, Sr., became the first black general in the U.S. Army. Benjamin O. Davis, Jr., his son, became a lieutenant general in the U.S. Air Force and the highest-ranking black in the military in 1965. At West Point in 1932, his classmates had refused to talk to him because of his race.

Such people have made Colin Powell's path easier. "We should be grateful," he once said, "for what all these men and women have done before. We cannot let the torch drop."

Blacks have a long history in the U.S. military. Top: A black regiment leads an attack during the Civil War. Left: World War II general Benjamin O. Davis, Sr. Right: Benjamin O. Davis, Jr., as an Air Force pilot.

After completing his training in 1958, Second Lieutenant Powell spent his first tour of duty in West Germany. As a platoon leader, he was in charge of forty men. His advice for all second lieutenants is: "Just take care of your soldiers. Too many young officers say, 'Gee, one of these days I'm going to be the chairman [of the JCS] or the chief of staff or I'm going to be a general.' I tell 'em, 'Oh, stop all that. Just go do the best you can and stop worrying about it.'"

Powell's second duty station was Fort Devens, Massachusetts. The year was 1960. By then he was a twenty-three-year-old first lieutenant. The army kept him busy, but he found time for racquetball, and for a blind date. She was Alma Vivian Johnson, the daughter of a high school principal from Birmingham, Alabama. She had a degree in audiology and taught students who were hearing impaired. Colin and Alma were married on August 25, 1962.

Early in the 1960s, the United States was sending military advisers to help the government of South Vietnam fight a Communist rebellion. It was the beginning of the Vietnam War. Powell, now a captain, spent 1963 as an adviser to a South Vietnamese infantry battalion. While he was there, he stepped in a trap that pierced his foot. He was out of action for a few weeks, and he won the Purple Heart. Later that year he was awarded the Bronze Star. By 1991 the general wore twenty-one decorations, six of them for combat.

The Powells' first child, Michael, was born while his father was in Vietnam. A daughter, Linda, was born in 1965, and a second daughter, Annemarie, was born about five years later.

When he came home from Vietnam, Powell was sent to the Army Command and General Staff College at Fort Leavenworth, Kansas. He asked an officer there about going to graduate school. "Your college grades aren't good enough," the officer said. That made Powell angry—and determined. When his Leavenworth class graduated, he was number 2 out of 1,244. How did he do it? Simple, the general recalled: "Hard work."

In 1968, Powell was a major, and he was back in Vietnam. A helicopter in which he was flying crashed and burned. Powell was thrown clear, but he ran back and pulled everyone to safety. For his

Soldiers emerge from a helicopter on a hilltop in Vietnam during the war there. Colin Powell served two tours of duty in Vietnam.

A Purple Heart, one of six combat decorations that Colin Powell earned during his career.

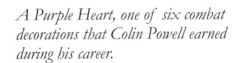

24

bravery, he was awarded the Soldier's Medal and another Bronze Star.

When he was back home again, Powell entered graduate school in Washington, D.C. He earned a master's degree in business administration from George Washington University in 1971.

Getting to the top in the military is a lot like getting to the top in any business. It doesn't hurt if the boss or the president knows your name. It doesn't hurt if people get to know how good you are. Powell's next move put him alongside some important people in the U.S. government. At the age of thirty-five, in 1972, he was one of seventeen military people picked to be special government assistants. They are called White House Fellows.

He served in the Office of Management and Budget. The deputy director of this office, Frank C. Carlucci, was very impressed with Major Colin Powell. The director, Caspar W. Weinberger, was also impressed. They both admired Powell's quiet efficiency and his competence. The three men became friends. This was important to Powell's future career.

But in 1973 it was time for overseas duty again.

Now a lieutenant colonel, Powell took command of the First Batallion, 32nd Infantry, in Korea. It was a unit torn by trouble. Blacks and whites didn't get along. Drug use was common. Powell later said that he "threw the bums out of the army and put the drug users in jail." But that wasn't all he did. After a few months, blacks and whites in the unit were working and living together without trouble. This experience made Powell deeply concerned about drug abuse, especially among young people.

After Korea, Powell began a chain of jobs that put him on a path straight to the top. He worked at the Defense Department, in Washington, D.C. He attended the National War College for advanced military schooling. He went to Fort Campbell, Kentucky, to command the Second Brigade, 101st Airborne Division. Then he returned to Washington, to work at the Defense Department and the Department of Energy.

His next posts were Fort Carson, Colorado, and Fort Leavenworth, Kansas, where he commanded some 18,000 soldiers. He rose higher and higher in the military chain of command. He was promoted to colonel, to brigadier general, and then to major general. By 1982 he wore two stars.

All this moving from place to place was hard for the Powells and their three children. Like many military families, they were very close. Powell spent as much time with his family as he could. He also tried to find time for his favorite hobby—fixing up old cars.

In 1983, Powell was called back to Washington once again. His old friends, Frank Carlucci and Caspar Weinberger, remembered him. He became the top military aide, first to Carlucci, who was now deputy secretary of defense, and then to Weinberger, secretary of defense in President Ronald Reagan's administration.

Weinberger came to depend more and more on his military aide. He admired the quiet, competent way in which General Powell ran the day-to-day workings of the giant Defense Department. Powell was able to get along with all kinds of people and to keep them all working together.

It wasn't easy. The United States had some bumpy times during those years. In 1983, U.S. troops

The Powell family, pictured in 1987. From the left are Annemarie, Michael, Linda, and Colin and Alma Powell.

invaded the Caribbean island of Grenada to restore order there. And 241 U.S. Marines were killed in a terrorist attack in Lebanon, in the Middle East.

Powell's work during this time brought him power and influence in the U.S. government. He earned a third star, becoming a lieutenant general. He also earned a job he had long wanted.

In the middle of 1986, Powell took over the U.S. Army Fifth Corps, headquartered in Frankfurt, Germany. This was his longtime dream of an infantry command. While he was in charge of this 75,000-member corps, he said he was "probably the happiest general in the world."

If so, it didn't last long. By the end of the year, Frank Carlucci was on the phone from Washington. The Reagan administration was in trouble over what became known as the Iran-contra scandal. Members of the administration were accused of selling weapons to Iran, ignoring a ban on such sales. They were also charged with supplying arms to rebels in Nicaragua. Congress had forbidden such action.

Carlucci wanted Powell to return to Washington and become the new national security adviser to President Reagan. The administration needed someone to help straighten things out.

The general politely said no. He had the job he wanted. He had earned it. He didn't want to leave.

Carlucci called twice more. Powell still said no. Then Carlucci told him, "The commander in chief needs you." By "commander in chief," he meant the president.

How could the general refuse? The next day President Ronald Reagan himself called. He said that he knew Powell wanted to stay in Germany. But, the president added, "We need you here."

The good soldier returned to the United States. Shortly after his return, he and his wife received tragic news. Their son, Michael, had been in an accident. At first doctors said he wouldn't live. Then they said he wouldn't walk. But he did both. It was a long recovery, but in time Michael was able to enter Georgetown University Law School in Washington, D.C. He married his college sweetheart, and they had the Powells' first grandchild, a boy named Jeffrey. In 1994, their second son, Bryan, was born.

General and Mrs. Powell's older daughter, Linda, became an actress in New York City. The youngest,

As national security adviser to President Ronald Reagan, Powell held an important job. Here he meets in the White House with (from left) Deputy Secretary of Defense Frank Carlucci, Secretary of State George Shultz, and President Reagan.

Annemarie, followed in her brother's and sister's footsteps and graduated from William and Mary College in Virginia.

Once back in the United States, the general's career continued to rise. As national security adviser, Powell proved to be the right man for the job. From December 1987 until January 1989, he kept things running smoothly between the White House and government agencies. He supervised important summit meetings between President Reagan and the leader of the Soviet Union, Mikhail Gorbachev.

No matter how big his job, the general always seemed to have time for people. At a White House dinner during Powell's last days as national security adviser, a black waiter said to him, "I know you're leaving. I just wanted to thank you and say that it's been good to see you here. I was in World War II, and I fought all the way from North Africa to Italy."

Powell replied, "Brother, I ought to be thanking you."

George Bush became president in January 1989. One of the first things he did was to put the genral out of a job. Bush told Powell that he wanted to name his own national security adviser. This is a common practice, and Powell understood. But even so, he began to wonder if the time had come to leave the army.

He talked it over with his family and close friends. Then, in his organized, precise way, he made up two lists: "Reasons to Leave the Army" and "Reasons to Stay in the Army." The "Leave" list had only one item: He could make about $1 million yearly just for giving lectures. The "Stay" list had many items. The most important one was simply that Colin Powell loved the army.

Powell stayed. He earned a fourth star, becoming a full general. Not many soldiers wear four stars in the U.S. Army. That is the top; ordinarily, you can't go higher. However, Congress can, and sometimes does, create the rank of five-star general. World War II heroes Dwight Eisenhower and Omar Bradley wore five stars.

Powell also got a new job in April 1989. He took over the U.S. Forces Command, at Fort McPherson, Georgia. To say that this was a big job is an understatement. He was in command of all troops stationed in the United States. That included some 250,000 active soldiers and 300,000 in the reserve and National Guard. His budget was $10 billion.

But bigger things were coming. Later that year, President Bush named Powell as the first African-American chairman of the Joint Chiefs of Staff.

The Joint Chiefs of Staff is an agency in the Department of Defense. It advises the president on military policy. The JCS has six members: the chairman, the vice chairman, the chiefs of staff of the army and the air force, the chief of naval operations, and the commandant of the Marine Corps. The group meets in Washington, D.C., three times a week, in a windowless room called "the tank." These six people decide on U.S. military matters. There are more than two million Americans in military service. Being chairman of the JCS is a big, and mostly top-secret, job.

The Powells moved to an elegant old house that is reserved for the chairman of the Joint Chiefs. It stands on a hill in Fort Myers, Virginia, a suburb of the nation's capital. The house has a grand view across the Potomac River. But the general joked that

Powell is sworn in as chairman of the Joint Chiefs of Staff on October 3, 1989. Secretary of Defense Dick Cheney administers the oath of office; Alma Powell is shown holding the Bible.

he sometimes longed for an army base, so that he could enjoy his hobby of fixing up old cars. Having old cars around the yard in Fort Myers, he said with a grin, "drags down the neighborhood."

As chairman of the Joint Chiefs, Powell had to handle a crisis almost immediately. On December 20, 1989, some 26,000 U.S. troops invaded the Central American country of Panama. They ousted Panama's dictator, Manuel Noriega, who was wanted in the United States on drug charges.

The biggest challenge was yet to come, however. More than anyone else, General Powell is given credit for the U.S. military success after Iraq refused to leave Kuwait in 1990–1991. The American military forces performed almost perfectly. From the start of the Persian Gulf War on January 16, allied planes bombed military and government facilities in Iraq. They were so accurate and thorough that when the ground war began, on February 24, Iraq surrendered in just one hundred hours.

The Persian Gulf War ended in a cease-fire on February 28, 1991. It had lasted just forty-three days. The United States and its allies had very few casualties. American men and women, weapons, and

Left: Tanks belonging to the 82nd Airborne Division move across the desert in Saudi Arabia. U.S. forces performed almost perfectly during the Persian Gulf War, and much of the credit went to Powell. Below: Powell visited the troops in Saudi Arabia in December 1990, just before the fighting broke out. Here he uses a soldier's head as a "writing desk" to sign an autograph.

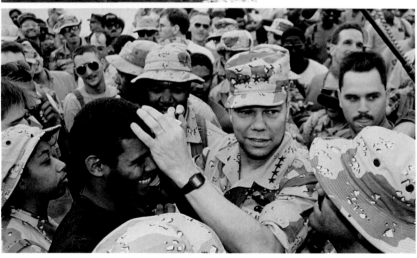

machines did such a good job that a wave of patriotism flooded the United States. Yellow ribbons (which stood for the hope that the troops would return safely) and American flags were everywhere, flying from houses, offices, and trees.

President Bush talked to Congress and the American people on March 6, 1991. "The war is over," he said. He gave credit for the battle plan and the smooth operation of the war to Colin Powell and to General H. Norman Schwarzkopf, who commanded the allied troops. There was even some talk of five stars for both men.

Obviously, George Bush was pleased with his choice for chairman of the Joint Chiefs of Staff. At the time Bush had named him, there were several men who had been generals longer than Powell had. Even so, no one had been really surprised at the president's choice. And, if anyone objected, no one had objected out loud. Instead, a Washington politician had said of the general: "I can't think of anyone who is critical of him."

President Bush nominated Powell for a second two-year term as chairman of the Joint Chiefs, and he was reconfirmed by the Senate in October 1991.

The following year, Powell headed the U.S. effort to feed the African nation of Somalia. About 25,000 American troops brought in food to people who were starving, mostly because of fighting among native warlords.

Bush lost the presidential election of 1992 to Democrat Bill Clinton. Where did that leave Powell? Rumors immediately started about his next career move. Would he leave the army at the end of his term as chairman? What about a career in politics?

Certainly, the general had plenty of fans to cheer him on whatever his choice. President Bush said, "It is most important that the chairman of the Joint Chiefs of Staff be a person of breadth, judgment, experience, and total integrity. Colin Powell has all these qualities and more."

Graham Claytor, former deputy defense secretary, was more direct. He said, "Colin would make a good president of the United States."

Many people agreed, but Colin Powell remained his usual quiet self. However, he had made one decision about his future. In September 1993, he retired from the United States Army after a distinguished thirty-five-year career.

Right after retirement, Powell began to write his autobiography. He crisscrossed the country giving speeches. In late 1994, President Clinton asked him to accompany former president Jimmy Carter on a peace mission to the Caribbean island nation of Haiti. The United States seemed on the verge of invading Haiti to topple the military dictatorship that had overthrown the elected president in 1991. Carter and Powell worked out an agreement, which led to the return of the rightful president and a peaceful solution.

The more Colin Powell said nothing, the more the rumors grew. Voices became louder in his support. Colin Powell for president! Colin Powell for vice president! Democrat? Republican? Is the nation ready for its first African-American commander in chief?

The distinguished former general—in civilian clothes now—was suddenly everywhere. At a bookstore in New York City, he signed copies of his autobiography, *My American Journey*. He was interviewed on television. Little by little, the public came to learn more about his political views. If he ran for office, it would be on the Republican ticket. He fa-

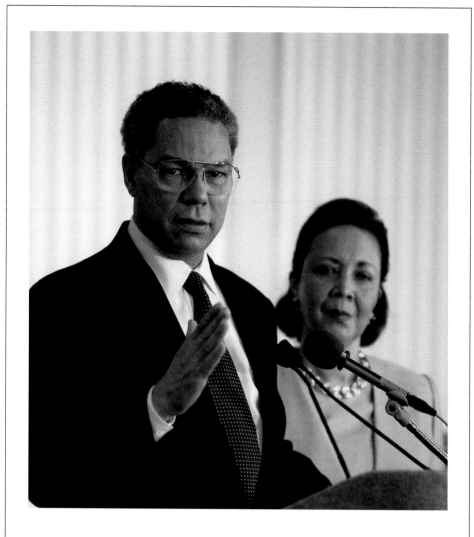

On November 8, 1995, with wife, Alma, by his side, Colin Powell announced that he would not run for president, putting an end to the rumors that had been circulating.

vored reducing the tax burden and the role of government in the private lives of citizens as much as possible. However, he also backed abortion laws and was very concerned about racial issues.

It seemed as though everyone in the country was awaiting Powell's decision. Would he run, or wouldn't he? The suspense finally ended on November 8, 1995. With his usual quiet graciousness, Colin Powell said no. He would not run. "Such a life," he said, "requires a calling that I do not yet hear."

Powell ruled out running for vice president, too. When asked if he would take a position as secretary of state, for example, he replied, "Nobody has offered me any offices, so I'm not going to rule anything in or out. But right now I intend to remain in private life." He added, "The future is the future."

But some people just didn't want to take no for an answer. One of them was Bob Dole, former senator from Kansas, who became the Republican party's choice to run for president in the 1996 election. Dole sought out Powell as a potential running mate. The general said no. Party leaders wanted Powell to take an active part in the campaign. The general said no. But he did agree to be a featured speaker at the

Republican National Convention in August 1996 in San Diego, California.

Colin Powell delivered a passionate speech that asked Republicans to be the "party of inclusion." He spoke of his vision of an America based on values, compassion, and fairness. He asked all Americans to work for the things that unite us and to remain devoted to the principles of freedom, democracy, and free enterprise. In closing, Powell urged the nation to believe in the promise of this country "where the best is always yet to come."

The general's speech once again left many people genuinely sorry that this respected American would not enter the political race in a more direct way. However, as others pointed out, Powell did not say never. He said that he did not yet hear the calling. He said, "The future is the future." There will be another presidential election in the year 2000. And the "Powell for President" buttons are still waiting to be worn.

IMPORTANT DATES

1937	April 5: Colin Luther Powell is born in Harlem, New York City.
1954	Graduates from Morris High School, Bronx, New York. Enters City College of New York.
1955	Joins ROTC unit at CCNY.
1958	Graduates from CCNY with a degree in geology. Commissioned second lieutenant in U.S. Army. Goes to Georgia for basic training. Sent on first tour of duty, in West Germany.
1960	Becomes first lieutenant. Sent to second duty station, Fort Devens, Massachusetts.
1963	Now a captain, Powell earns Purple Heart in Vietnam.
1968	Now a major, second tour of duty in Vietnam.
1971	Earns master's degree in business administration, George Washington University, Washington, D.C.
1972	Named White House Fellow.

1973	Now a lieutenant colonel, tour of duty in Korea.
1974	Serves tour of duty in Washington, D.C.
1975	Attends National War College, in Washington, D.C.
1976	Now a colonel, sent to Fort Campbell, Kentucky.
1977–1982	Holds various posts and achieves rank of major general.
1983–1986	Serves as military aide to secretary of defense. Becomes a lieutenant general.
1986	Takes command of Army Fifth Corps, Frankfurt, Germany.
1987–1989	Serves as national security adviser, Reagan administration.
1989	April 4: Earns four stars. October 1: Named chairman of Joint Chiefs of Staff.
1990–1991	Oversees successful operation of Persian Gulf War.
1992	Leads U.S. effort to bring food to starving people of Somalia.
1993	September: Retires from U.S. Army after thirty-five-year career.
1994	Accompanies Jimmy Carter to Haiti on peace mission.
1995	Publishes autobiography, *My American Journey*. November 8: Announces decision not to run for presidency.
1996	August: Is featured speaker at Republican National Convention in San Diego, California.

INDEX